Koalas

Koalas

Library of Congress Cataloging-in-Publication Data
Lee, Sandra.
Koalas / by Sandra Lee.
p.   cm.
Includes index.
Summary: Describes the physical characteristics,
behavior, habitat, and life cycle of the koala.
ISBN 1-56766-396-6 (lib. reinforced : alk. paper)
1. Koala—Juvenile literature.   [1. Koala.]   I. Title
QL737.M384L435   1998
599.2'5—dc21   97-30410
                            CIP
                            AC

Photo Credits

ANIMALS ANIMALS © Hans & Judy Beste: 9
© Art Wolfe/Tony Stone Images: 19, 20, 26
© Comstock, Inc.: 13
© 1993 DPA/Dembinsky Photo Assoc. Inc.: 10
© 1994 Mark J. Thomas/Dembinsky Photo Assoc. Inc.: 23, 30
© 1997 Martin Withers/Dembinsky Photo Assoc. Inc.: cover
© 1995 Martin Withers/Dembinsky Photo Assoc. Inc.: 24
© Matthew Lambert/Tony Stone Images: 2
© Robert and Linda Mitchell: 15, 29
© Russ Kinne/Comstock, Inc.: 6
© Tony Stone Worldwide: 16

On the cover...

Front cover: This koala is watching the things around him.
Page 2: This koala is sitting in a tree in Australia.

Table of Contents

There are many strange animals on Earth. Some of them look funny. Others make odd noises. Some do very unusual things. Each of these creatures is interesting in its own way. And one of the most interesting is the koala!

⇐ This koala is resting in a tree.

What Are Koalas?

Many people think koalas are bears, but that is not true. Koalas belong to a group of animals called **marsupials**. Kangaroos and opossums are marsupials, too. Marsupials are animals that have a pocket of skin for carrying their babies. This pocket is called a **pouch**. Only female marsupials have pouches. A female koala's pouch is on the front of her stomach.

This mother koala is carrying her baby in her pouch. ⇒

What Do Koalas Look Like?

Koalas are covered with thick, gray fur. The fur is thick enough to be almost waterproof! Koalas have big ears that are covered with hair. They also have cheek pouches for holding food. Koalas even have a tail—but it is almost too short to see. Most adult koalas are two feet tall and weigh about 20 pounds.

⇐ Koalas like this one have thick, soft fur.

Koalas might look like quiet animals, but they are really very noisy. They grunt when they eat. They whine loudly when they are scared. Many people think they sound like a human baby crying.

These koalas are talking to each other. ⇒

What Are Baby Koalas Like?

Like other marsupial babies, a newborn koala is very tiny—it is only as big as a honeybee! The newborn cannot see or hear. It has no fur on its body. But it does have strong front legs for crawling. Right after it is born, the baby koala crawls into its mother's pouch.

Once the baby is inside the pouch, it hangs onto something that looks like a little finger. This is called a **teat**. Milk from the mother's body comes out of the teat. That is what the baby drinks while it is inside the pouch. Slowly, the baby koala grows bigger and stronger. After about six months, it is ready to leave the pouch.

A newborn koala would look very much like this newborn *opossum*. ⇒

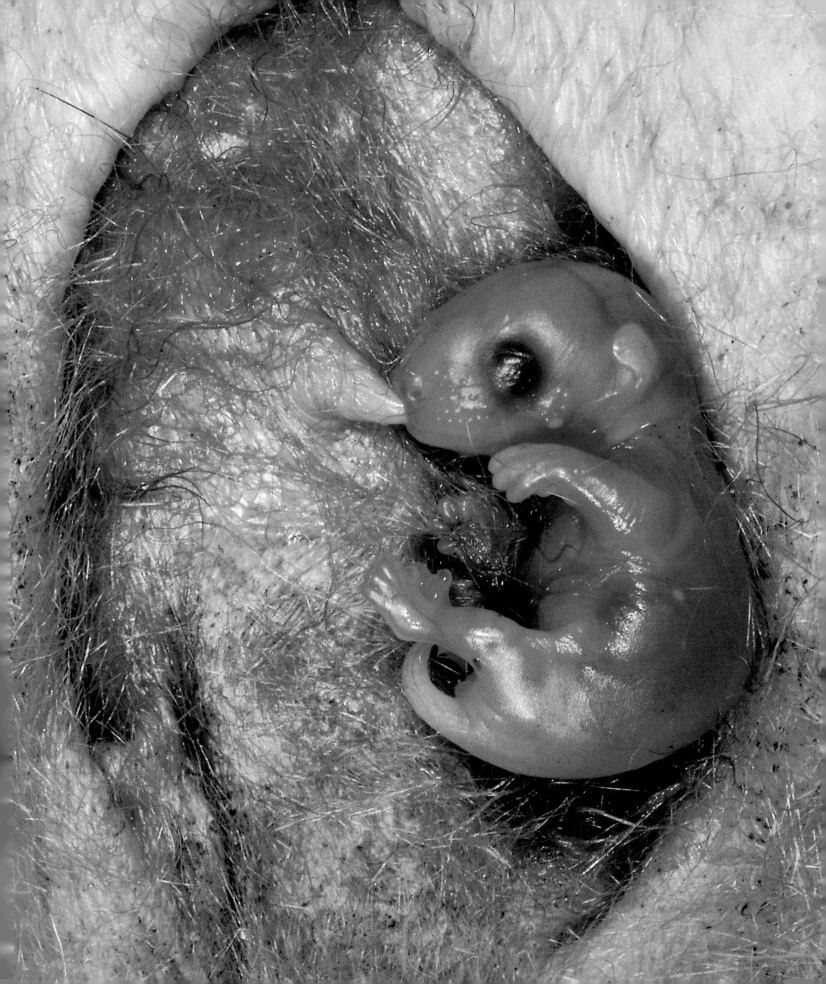

After it leaves the pouch, the young koala stays very close to its mother. It rides on the mother's head or back wherever she goes. If it is sleepy or afraid, the baby climbs back into the pouch. When it is about a year old, the young koala leaves its mother and finds its own place to live.

Where Do Koalas Live?

Koalas live only in the eastern parts of Australia. They live in *eucalyptus* (yoo-cuh-LIP-tus) trees. A koala's body is perfect for life in the trees. Each of its hands has two thumbs. These thumbs are ideal for grabbing branches. Sharp claws on the koala's hands and feet also help it to climb.

It is easy to see why koalas are such good climbers. ⇒

Koalas are very fussy eaters. In fact, all they eat is eucalyptus leaves! There are many kinds of eucalyptus trees, but koalas eat only a few types. They are even fussy about which leaves they eat! Before they eat a leaf, they carefully check and smell it. If it isn't quite right, they throw it away.

⇐ This koala is munching on leaves.

Koalas aren't very active. They spend most of the day sleeping in the trees. When a koala moves, it looks as if it is in slow motion. Why don't koalas have a lot of energy? It is because of their food. Eucalyptus leaves do not provide very much energy, so the koalas move slowly.

Koalas like this one spend a lot of time sleeping. ⇒

Eucalyptus leaves do provide a lot of water, though. In fact, they hold almost all the water a koala needs to drink. Every once in a while, the koala might climb down to the ground for a drink. But it doesn't stay on the ground for long! As soon as it can, it climbs back up into the safety of the trees.

Do Koalas Have Any Enemies?

Koalas spend almost all of their lives high in the treetops. There they are safe from most enemies. Sometimes, however, koalas are attacked by large owls or giant lizards. Wild dogs called **dingoes** also eat koalas if they find them on the ground.

⇐ Dingoes like this one sometimes eat koalas.

The koalas' worst enemies are humans. By building houses and cities, people are destroying many areas where koalas live. Farmers have cut down many eucalyptus forests to make more cropland. Without eucalyptus trees, the koalas cannot survive.

This koala is trying to stay safe by hiding in a treetop. ⇒

The people of Australia are now trying to protect the koalas. They have set aside special areas with plenty of eucalyptus trees for the koalas to live in. These special areas are called **preserves**. In the preserves, the koalas are safe from farmers and builders. The eucalyptus trees are safe, too. If people continue to take care of Australia's eucalyptus forests, koalas will be munching leaves for a long, long time.

Glossary

dingoes (DING-ohz)
Dingoes are wild dogs that live in Australia. Dingoes sometimes eat koalas that climb down to the ground.

marsupial (mar-SOO-pee-ull)
A marsupial is an animal that carries its young in a pouch. Koalas, kangaroos, and opossums are all marsupials.

pouch (POWCH)
A pouch is a pocket of skin where marsupial babies live. It is on the mother's stomach.

preserves (pre-ZURVZ)
Preserves are special areas where things are protected. In Australia, preserves have been set aside to protect koalas and eucalyptus trees.

teat (TEET)
A koala mother produces milk from two teats. They are like baby bottles inside the koala's pouch.

Index